W9-BNG-158

RG

Entrepreneurial
Smarts

Diane Bailey

ROSEN
PUBLISHING®

New York

Published in 2013 by The Rosen Publishing Group, Inc.
29 East 21st Street, New York, NY 10010

Copyright © 2013 by The Rosen Publishing Group, Inc.

First Edition

Library of Congress Cataloging-in-Publication Data

Bailey, Diane, 1966–
Entrepreneurial smarts/Diane Bailey.—1st ed.
    p. cm.—(Get smart with your money)
Includes bibliographical references and index.
ISBN 978-1-4488-8253-3 (library binding)—
ISBN 978-1-4488-8264-9 (pbk.)—
ISBN 978-1-4488-8265-6 (6-pack)
1. Entrepreneurship. 2. Small business—Management. I. Title.
HB615.B347 2013
658—dc23

                                                    2012023108

Manufactured in the United States of America

CPSIA Compliance Information: Batch #W13YA: For further information, contact Rosen Publishing, New York, New York, at 1-800-237-9932.

Contents

Introduction

When you run your own business, you choose what you do. You set your own hours. You don't have to answer to someone else. In short, you're in charge. That's the good part, anyway. The other side to being in charge is that *you're in charge*. What you decide can make or break your company and determine your success.

Making smart choices in terms of what you do; when, where and how you do it; whom you hire (if anyone); and of course, how you manage your finances, will have a huge impact on your business. Entrepreneurs have to worry about money in ways that traditional employees don't. It's not just your salary that's at stake; it's the financial stability of the whole company.

Still, the reason to go into business for yourself should not be about money, money, money. It's not very satisfying to do something you hate. It's great to have financial goals, but they should come second to doing something you like.

Some entrepreneurs have become household names. Perhaps you've heard of Bill Gates or Steve Jobs? Both were computer geeks first and successful businessmen second. Walt Disney was an artist who drew a cute mouse named Mickey before he started the company that eventually became known for family

Apple Computer's Steve Jobs *(left)* and Microsoft's Bill Gates *(right)* joined forces at this 1985 meeting. The two firms are powerful players in the personal computer industry.

entertainment. Henry Ford worked as an engineer at Thomas Edison's company, where he liked to tinker with gasoline engines. Ford combined that interest with the revolutionary idea of assembly line manufacturing. That led to the first mass-produced automobile, a development that changed the face of America.

Fortunately, you're more likely to be successful—financially and otherwise—at something you enjoy and are good at doing. However, many entrepreneurs have failed even though they were good at making their products or providing their services. Their downfall? They simply didn't know how to handle the business end of things in order to run a profitable company.

It all boils down to one simple rule: you've got to make more than you spend. However, understanding the costs involved with a business, and how to manage them, takes a little education and practice. Today's successful entrepreneurs know they can't compete without any knowledge of income, expenses, or the cost of doing business. That doesn't mean that other professionals, such as lawyers or accountants, can't help out. In fact, as your business becomes more complex, turning to experts can be a good idea. But until that time comes, it's important to have a basic understanding of how a company makes and spends money.

Part of this means mastering some basic math skills so that you can keep accurate records of how your company is performing financially. Other financial "smarts" come under the heading of thinking like a businessperson: finding ways to increase your profits, saving money where you can, and knowing when and where you should spend the money you have. The key to entrepreneurism is using your business savvy to give your business the best possible chance in a competitive world.

CHAPTER 1
Setting the Course

While it's important not to dive into entrepreneurism *only* for financial reasons, making money is nonetheless a worthy goal. After all, if you're going to start a business, then you probably want to earn enough to continue doing it.

Choosing a Business

Maybe you already know what you want to do. You're a lawn-mowing fiend and want to turn it into a full-service landscaping business. Perhaps everyone is clamoring for one of your famous hand-knitted scarves. Maybe you've hit upon an idea for an online business that will make Amazon.com look like a little mom-and-pop corner store. If this is the case, you're likely thinking about how you can generate an income from your passion. Taking a hobby or interest you already enjoy—from babysitting to photography to performing—has been the seed of many businesses.

On the other hand, you might not have a perfectly clear idea what you want to do. You like

A teenager who enjoys outdoor activities could decide to turn chores such as lawn mowing, gardening, and other yard work into a profitable part-time business.

the idea of working for yourself, but as it happens, you'd be happy mowing lawns *or* knitting scarves. Which to choose?

This is where market research proves useful. Good entrepreneurs are skilled at evaluating the market and finding where pieces are missing. They see what needs aren't being met—and how people will pay for those needs to be satisfied. There may be all kinds of things that you enjoy and are good at doing. However, there may be only a handful that could

Values

Personal values play a part in choosing the right business. If your religion forbids working on Saturday or Sunday, then selling goods at a flea market may be a problem, since those are the days most people go shopping. If you're passionate about preserving the environment, you might even reject the idea of a lemonade stand because you would use too many disposable cups. On the other hand, many entrepreneurs have built businesses that promote their values. In 1970, Tom Chappell and his wife, Kate, invested $5,000 to start Tom's of Maine, a business that makes personal care products, such as toothpaste. The products are made with natural ingredients, use packaging that can be recycled, and are not tested on animals.

translate into successful businesses. Perhaps you can sell your scarf for $20. However, the yarn costs $6, and it takes you seven hours to make it. That means you're earning a measly $2 an hour, just to break even! Overall, knitting scarves won't be the most lucrative business, unless you can find a way to cut costs, improve your efficiency, raise your prices, or some combination of all three.

The Big Picture

Entrepreneurs thrive in capitalist economies, which means that any individual or company has the right to try to make

People wait in line to buy Apple's iPad tablet as soon as it is released. Apple successfully identified what its customers wanted and created a product that satisfied them.

money through ideas and hard work—as long as it's legal, of course. The cornerstone of these kinds of economies is the market. At its most basic, a market is divided into two camps: people who provide goods or services, and people who consume them. Supply and demand, and how these two forces influence one another, drives the market.

Several things affect how the two act together. For example, if there is very little of a product, but a lot of people want it, the price goes up as people compete to see who "wins" the right to buy it. If there's a huge amount of something, then a supplier might lower the price to encourage people to buy it so that he's not stuck with a lot of unsold inventory.

The same principle applies to services. Two businesses might offer haircuts. One charges $10 and the other charges $40. The lower-priced business might get more business. However, the $40 haircut also comes with a consultation, a shampoo and styling, and fancy bottled water and cookies as well. These two vendors have now found separate niches in the market. One provides a low-cost alternative, while the other concentrates on customers who are willing to pay more for additional services. A business might establish itself by being the cheapest, the fastest, the fanciest, or something else entirely, but a key component of entrepreneurship is finding a niche. Ideally, this is a specific segment of the market that is not being served or that could be served better with a different approach.

Entrepreneurs sometimes talk about turning caterpillars (ideas) into butterflies (successful businesses). When evaluating the potential of a business, several factors should be considered. Does the idea fulfill a need in the market? Is there a way it can effectively compete—in other words, even if it's similar to something else out there, can it offer an advantage? Can the idea be developed and offered in a time frame that's fast enough to take advantage of the gap

Ignoring the Experts

Western Union wasn't worried. In the late 1800s, an internal memo from the telegraph company read: "This 'telephone' has too many shortcomings to be seriously considered as a means of communication. The device is inherently of no value to us." The company didn't see the value of a telephone, but other people sure did! In 1899, the director of the U.S. Patent Office declared, "Everything that can be invented has been invented." Um, MP3 player, anyone? Some of the best entrepreneurs have been visionaries. Their ideas were so revolutionary, so ahead of their time, that their contemporaries thought they were crazy. How could it possibly work? Although it's important to consider the viability of an idea in the current market, it's also important to believe in your idea.

in the market? Finally, how likely is the business to continue to succeed and be profitable over time?

Setting Goals

You've likely stayed up late studying for a test, or spent an extra hour practicing your piano for a recital or your fast pitch for a big game. Why? You had a goal. You wanted to get a good grade, impress your audience, or beat the opposing team. Otherwise, you would not have had as much incentive to put in the work. The same applies to a business.

It's important to determine what your goals are. Some of these might be financial. If you're just trying to earn some extra spending money, some occasional babysitting or a part-time job at the grocery store might do the trick. If you're trying to put yourself through college, then you might decide you need a job that's going to pay better, and that the way to achieve that is with your own business.

You might also be using your business to develop your skills or opportunities. For example, if you mow enough lawns, you can work on building a customer base from which you can draw when you branch out into general landscaping. You might not earn a lot right now, but you're still using your business to achieve a long-term financial goal.

When you're setting your goals, decide what you want in several categories. What kind of work will satisfy you? How do you want your job to be structured? How much money do you want to earn?

Consider the costs you'll encounter along the way as well. Some businesses require very little start-up money. A tutoring business could begin on a shoestring budget. Print some business cards and a few fliers to advertise your services, and you're good to go. Chances are, your academic

Building a customer base is an important part of establishing any business. Simple publicity techniques such as distributing business cards can help spread the word.

skills are already up to snuff, or you wouldn't have chosen this business in the first place; you won't have to spend time or money acquiring new knowledge or skills. And you won't need to pay any employees, unless you're going to hire your smart friends to help out.

A lawn-mowing business, on the other hand, might run you a little more. You might need to buy a mower or figure out transportation to faraway jobs. Specialized businesses, such as Web design, could require you to invest in expensive software. And you might need to acquire the skill. You might have to pay for a class, but even if you don't, there will be a hidden expense in the time it takes to learn. Of course, this doesn't mean you shouldn't pursue it, but it's important to remember that some things will take longer to make money at than others.

CHAPTER 2

Creating a Business Plan

Great ideas are the foundations of great businesses, and hard work builds the walls. But those aren't enough. You also need a plan of how to build and grow a business. You have to know where you're starting, where you want to go, and most importantly, how you're going to get there. A business plan can help you identify your assets, define your needs, and set your goals. It also serves as a tool you can use to convince other people to invest in your business.

The Parts of a Business Plan

A business plan can run from just a few pages to many hundreds, depending on the complexity of the prospective company. At the heart is a description of the product or service being offered, as well as the company's overall vision. These sections are designed to sell the concept of the business, to show off its inherent "good idea"-ness.

Next, a business plan should include a marketing plan and strategy. This section describes the company's target market, describing the

A good business plan clearly outlines the purpose and mission of a particular business, as well as the particulars of how it will operate.

projected size of its customer base and explaining what those customers are like. It also includes information on competitors and how the new company will fit into the existing market.

How is everything going to work? That's what's covered in the operations portion of the business plan. The nitty-gritty of producing and distributing a product is discussed here. Now, who's in charge? An entrepreneur may start the business and direct its basic vision, but no company runs itself. Large companies (and many small ones) depend on the work and talents of many people. If you're just starting out, you may not be thinking "management team" or "board of directors." Nonetheless, it's a good idea to consider who's doing

Types of Businesses

Businesses can be structured in a variety of ways. The legal organization of a company depends on what type of business it is and how it's run. A sole proprietorship is run by a single person. The business might not even have its own bank account, but instead operates through the proprietor's personal finances. A partnership involves two or more people. General partners usually have day-to-day responsibilities for running the business, as well as a financial stake. Limited partners have only financial involvement. Corporations have other tax and legal requirements. Generally, corporations pay more taxes. However, if a company faces legal trouble, the corporate structure helps protect the people who operate the business from being personally liable.

what and what other people you may need to depend on, whether they be employees, suppliers, or professionals who will provide specialized services.

Also consider how long it will take to get everything up and running. Market niches often open and close relatively quickly. There can't be too long a gap between when a need is identified and when it can be fulfilled.

Financial Considerations

With the overall vision of a company's purpose in place, the next step is to develop a concrete idea of how much money a company will make, how much it will need, and how to pay for everything. You've likely had to figure out how to use your allowance or birthday money. If you have $50, are you going to save it, buy a video game, or buy fifty packs of gum? It's your money—you can do what you want. But if you're starting a business, it might not be your money—at least not all of it—so it's important to prove that the business has a strong financial footing. That means enough money to get things started, as well as enough to keep them going.

Start-up costs loom in front of every business, and they are the first financial hurdle to clear. For some businesses—such as a tutoring service—these may be relatively low. If you're planning on selling handmade crafts, then you may need to invest in materials. Again, however, these can be kept low if you're starting small. Service-based businesses, in general, require less money at the outset.

Other businesses, however, can have huge initial costs. Manufacturing tractors doesn't come cheap. You'll need heavy machinery. Lots of materials. Storage space. People to do the job. The payoff may be a lot higher: if you can sell ten tractors for $100,000 each, that will help pay for the start-up costs. The

A retail business selling products, such as the supplies shown in this craft store, will require more money to get started in order to build inventory.

trick is getting there. Businesses that require a lot of money up front will likely require outside investment, which is where the other parts of the business plan come into play. It's OK to be ambitious, and it's OK to dream, but a hefty dose of realism often means the difference between a successful business and a failed one.

After start-up costs are accounted for, it's time to make some projections. What costs will there be in the first few months? A year? Five years? What are the projected sales figures? Try to anticipate variations in your business, such as seasonal fluctuations. Now put together a projected income statement, also called a profit and loss statement. This will detail what your expenses will be and how much income you expect.

Mark Your Territory

Got a great idea? You might want to make sure no one steals it. Certain types of "intellectual property," such as pieces of writing or music, are automatically protected under copyright law as soon as they are created. Other things require a more formal process. If you've invented a great product that you want to sell—and you want to make sure no one copies you—you can register for a patent with the U.S. Patent Office. If your application is approved, your idea will be protected so that, for a certain number of years, only you (or someone you designate) have the right to use it.

Marking the Milestones

Many businesses do not make money the first year. Lots of them don't make money for several years. As long as this

scenario is accounted for in your business plan, a lag in time isn't necessarily a deal-breaker. Some ideas need time to develop a technology or customer base. Amazon.com made its first sale in 1995, but the company didn't turn a profit until 2001. However, the company had written a business plan that embraced slow, but more stable, growth. When many online companies went under during the dot.com "bust" of the late 1990s, Amazon held on. Today, it is the largest online retailer in the world.

Every business is different. The people who generate the idea, the people who run the company, and the customers who use it, all have their own goals and requirements. While there are guidelines to establishing a company's financial operations, these are affected by the unique circumstances of the business itself.

Setting goals will help keep things on track. Define both short-term and long-term goals. Decide where the company ought to be in six months, a year, and even five years. Create manageable—and achievable—goals. Sure, you might want to make a million dollars in your first year, but

Selling everything from books to boxing gloves, the online retailer Amazon.com is a household name. Founder Jeff Bezos celebrates the company's ten-year anniversary in 2005.

unless you've really stumbled onto the Next Big Thing, that's only setting yourself up for failure.

A better approach is to create goals that aren't strictly about money but that tie into the overall financial performance of the company. For example, if you're selling handmade necklaces, rather than setting a goal to earn $1,000 in a year, you might set a goal to make ten necklaces a month and find two good markets to sell them.

Remember, though, that some businesses can start with a bang, but then fizzle out. At first, the customer base hasn't been tapped at all. For the first six months, it might be relatively easy to sell necklaces to friends and relatives. But where do you turn after that? It's important to plan for the next stage.

Chapter 3

Finding Financing

The old saying "You have to spend money to make money" was probably first uttered by an entrepreneur. A lightbulb may go off in your head with a good idea, but at some point, it will be time to pay the electric bill.

Sources of Financing

It's possible you have a couple million bucks that are giving your piggy bank a stomachache. However, it's more likely that if you need a significant amount of money, you'll be facing that first entrepreneurial hurdle: raising some cash. Financing comes in two major categories: debt and equity. Debt financing means taking out a loan, or borrowing money that must be paid back. Equity financing is a way to raise money by offering a financial stake in the company, such as stock shares.

Yourself, Friends, and Family

A large percentage of entrepreneurs tap the most obvious cash source first—themselves. Your

Often, starting a business starts at home. Financial help from friends and family has helped many new businesses succeed during the difficult first years.

own savings can help finance the business. Investors often look favorably on entrepreneurs who are willing to put up some of their own money because it shows a real commitment to making the business work. You can also ask family members or friends to lend you money. If you take out a loan from them, be sure to set the terms. Decide what the interest rate will be, as well as when you will be required to pay it back. The advantage to borrowing from people you know is that they might be willing to help out when a bank is not. A disadvantage is that if you have trouble repaying the loan, it can lead to hard feelings and put a strain on your personal relationships. In addition, a loan may make these people feel entitled to put their "fingers in the pot" and try to tell you how to run your business.

Banks and Lenders

Borrowing money from a bank or other lender follows some basic principles. The amount is paid back over a certain time period, with extra added on for interest. While banks are in the business of lending money, this doesn't mean they'll hand it out without some safeguards in place. People and businesses sometimes default on their loans—meaning they don't have the money to pay them back—and then the bank loses money. To ensure against this, banks look for businesses that have a solid footing and a promising future. This is where the business plan comes into play. An entrepreneur improves his chances of getting a loan if he can demonstrate that his business is likely to succeed. A bank might also require some collateral—something that the borrower can put up in exchange for the loan. If a borrower puts up his car as collateral and fails to repay the loan, then the bank can seize the vehicle and sell it to settle the debt. The rules and requirements vary, so be sure you understand all the particulars. Credit card debt is another type of loan, but it's expensive and best avoided. Also, people under age eighteen cannot legally get a credit card.

Certain businesses qualify for special loans. Government loans exist for businesses that are working to develop new technologies or products from which the government could benefit. The Small Business Administration (SBA) is a government agency that specializes in funneling money to small businesses. Women, members of minority groups, and teen entrepreneurs also can apply for loans targeted specifically to them.

Investors

Some people may not have their own business, but they like the idea of being involved in someone else's. Investors buy into businesses for several reasons. They might personally know the entrepreneur and want to help her. They may feel that aligning themselves with the new business is smart

Investors, like these venture capitalists, are always on the lookout for new business concepts. Entrepreneurs present their ideas in hopes of attracting money to fund their businesses.

networking that will help them in other business ventures. Other times, their motivation is purely financial. Venture capitalists invest money (capital) into a new business (venture).

The Answer's "No"

It's easy enough to go to the bank and fill out a loan application. It's not too difficult to present a business plan to an investor. But it's harder to convince someone to say "yes." Certainly, a bank will make money if a loan is repaid, and an investor could get rich if a company takes off. But there's always a risk. Financiers weigh the potential rewards against the risks that are being assumed. Sometimes they don't feel it's worth it. Most entrepreneurs have heard "no" from time to time. If this happens, try someone else. If the "no" answers persist, however, it's time to reevaluate the plan. Is the amount of money you're requesting reasonable? Does the business plan accurately state the company's objectives and operations? Are the income projections realistic? Lenders and investors usually have good reasons for saying "no." If you don't know what those reasons are, ask! Then make the appropriate changes.

Financing isn't a onetime event. Instead, as a company's monetary needs change, so does the process for acquiring more funds. An entrepreneur will have to evaluate her company's needs at different stages. What will it need in the first few months? The first year? At what point does she expect income to cover expenses—the break-even point? How much money will be reinvested to grow the business, which may require additional financing to cover immediate costs?

Raising money tends to take longer than expected, so when you're budgeting costs, be sure to budget enough time to find financing as well!

Instead of providing traditional loans, venture capitalists negotiate an agreement that lets them profit from the company—if the company does profit, that is. This type of investing comes with a relatively large degree of risk. The idea may be good—but will it work? Markets and customers can be unpredictable. In addition, even if the business idea shows promise, will the people running it be up to the job? Again, a thorough business plan is the first line of defense in proving the worth of a business. Angel investors are another type of venture capitalist, but they can be a little harder to find. These are generally individuals who like to invest in new companies, but they're not formally associated with a firm.

Do the Due

It's expected—and smart—to do some research in preparation of investing money. Before committing funds, an investor will probably look at the viability of a new company's idea, as well as check out the people who will be running things. The investor will make sure the business has a sensible approach to operating, and thus a reasonable chance of success. This process is called due diligence. It works both ways. Entrepreneurs should learn about their potential investors. What is the investor's track record? What's the motivation for becoming involved with your company? How does this investor work—and more to the point, will you be able to work together? Besides investing money, what other ways can the investor help the company? Legitimate investors want your company to succeed—their success is tied to yours. If they want too much for what they're giving, walk away.

Evaluating the Choices

Depending on the type of business, as well as the goals of the entrepreneur, one type of financing may be preferable to another. Some may not be options at all. Several factors influence the process.

As an entrepreneur, determine how much control you want to keep over your company. With traditional loans, you retain ownership of the company—as long as the loan is paid back. (If it's not, the bank often has the right to take your assets.) Equity financing—giving investors a stake in the company in return for

Large commercial banks may lend money to entrepreneurs who want to start a business, although they often are more conservative than private investors. Do some research before approaching a bank for a loan.

their money—means that you will give up some ownership and control of the company. It won't be all yours anymore.

The nature of the business often determines what type of financing is needed. Banks, in general, are more conservative in their lending and are unwilling to take as many risks as a venture capitalist. A company with huge start-up costs may be forced to turn to investors in order to get the money. Likewise, a business with a cutting-edge, but risky, premise may need to depend on venture financing.

Some businesses also qualify for grants—onetime gifts from a government or private agency. Grants are a fund-raiser's dream, but usually there is a lot of competition for them.

It's also important to consider how much to borrow. Some experts advise borrowing only what you need. Others recommend trying for a little more. What's the "right" decision? Often, it depends on the business and how you'll be running it. Debt costs money. More debt costs more money. That's an argument to stay away from assuming more than is necessary. On the other hand, borrowing more than you think you'll need can give you a cushion to get through tough times. It's likely you won't have full control over this decision. Even if you want to borrow $5,000, a bank might approve only a $3,000 loan. It's also important to remember that different kinds of debt cost different amounts. A bank might charge 8 percent interest on a loan. A credit card will charge double that, or more.

Think carefully about how much to ask for. Too little, and you may cripple your chances of success. Too much, and you could appear as if you're not being careful with your money. Also, in the case of equity financing, if you trade away too much, you could lessen your control over the company.

Myths & Facts

Myth If an investor wants to invest in your company, there's no reason to say "no"—money is money!

Fact You may have to work closely with your investors, so choose someone who has a similar outlook and goals. People who can bring contacts or skills to your company can be more valuable as those who bring only money.

Myth A great idea is a great idea. It doesn't matter when a business gets started if the product will "sell itself."

Fact Markets are fickle. Successful entrepreneurs are skilled at reading the market and determining when the time is right for a product or service to be able to profit.

Myth People under eighteen don't have to pay taxes.

Fact Tax liability is determined by income, not age. If you earn a certain minimum amount, you must file a return with the Internal Revenue Service (IRS).

Chapter 4

Day to Day

Two challenges for any entrepreneur—once he or she has gotten some money—are using it wisely and understanding where it's going. This doesn't mean that you have to master the ins and outs of advanced accounting, but basic bookkeeping skills are a must. Learning to keep accurate records will show what's coming in, what's going out, and what changes need to be made.

Creating an Income Statement

Very few people, entrepreneurs or otherwise, have enough money to spend on everything they want. Money doesn't grow on trees, on bushes, or in flower beds. The first step in a business might be getting the idea, but the first *financial* step is creating a budget.

First, determine the cost of any materials you'll need. Estimate your per-unit cost. For example, for a scarf-knitting business, you'll need to buy yarn. If it takes two skeins of yarn to make a scarf, at a price of $5 each, then your materials cost per scarf is $10. (If you can afford to buy in bulk, you might get a discount.)

When planning a new business, it's important to consider start-up costs and ongoing expenses, such as money that must be spent to buy supplies.

Next, look at the cost of any equipment you'll need. Perhaps you already own a pair of knitting needles to start out with. However, frenzied weekends of knitting might wear them out. Budget to buy a new pair in a few months, if necessary. For some businesses, you may need to buy equipment at the outset. That lawn-mowing business might not last too long if you have to depend on the old clunky mower in the garage. If you can't afford to buy a mower before launching your business, you might decide to save a portion of the money you make from each job to buy a new one.

Consider the general expenses of actually running your business. Indirect costs are called overhead. A telephone, office equipment and supplies, rent, insurance, licenses or permits, and utilities all might come into play. Factor in marketing and publicity costs, such as printing business cards or fliers, or advertising. You might also need to budget in the cost of repaying any loans you've taken out or paying employees. Some expenses can be amortized, or spread out over time. For example, a $600 computer can be spread out to $50 a month for a year. If you have a small business, you might be operating out of your bedroom and not have all these expenses at first, but they may arise as your business grows.

Next, record your income. If you can make two scarves per week and sell each for $20, that's $40 per week. That figure goes on the other side of the paper. Don't forget to consider the cost of your time. At first, you might work a lot of hours for little pay, but this shouldn't be a long-term strategy.

Some businesses expect to lose money at the beginning because they need time to get established. Obviously, though, at some point the income line needs to be bigger than the expenses line. Your gross profit is the total amount of money you make. Subtract your expenses from this number to determine your net profit. That's the number that shows whether or not you're making money.

Keeping Records

When you are writing your business plan, your costs and expenses will only be estimates. Once you start operating the business, you can plug in the real numbers. It's vital to keep track of your actual expenses. Making a plan helps

Basic bookkeeping skills are a must for any entrepreneur. It's important to understand how a business is making money and where it is spending it.

prepare you, but reality sometimes has its own ideas. Know what you're spending, and what you're earning. If possible, get bookkeeping software to make the job easier.

It's also important to separate your income statement from your cash flow statement. The income statement shows your income and expenses; however, these numbers don't necessarily add up to what's really going on. For example, you might have billed out $100—a figure that you can put on an income statement—but until you are paid, it would not go on the cash flow statement. That statement shows actual money collected and spent.

Create a paper trail. When billing your customers, create an invoice showing the date of the transaction and the total due. Keep receipts for things you purchase. (That's what old shoeboxes are for.) If you forget to log something, you'll still have the receipt, and when it comes time to pay taxes, you may need your original records.

It's a good idea to open a bank account that you can use specifically for your business. Get a checkbook to pay your bills—the check becomes a built-in record. Use deposit slips to keep track of what you got paid for. When your bank statement arrives, check it against your own records to make sure they match.

If your earnings reach a certain amount, you will also have to pay taxes. Self-employed people must pay an additional tax that would ordinarily be covered by their employers. If you are selling a product, you are obligated to collect the proper amount of sales tax and then pass it on to the government. Many business expenses are tax deductible, meaning that you can subtract them from the amount of income that is taxed (not from the total due). Large pieces of equipment can be depreciated over time. While you can't deduct the entire expense at once, things wear out, and you can take a little bit off each year. You can also reduce the amount of tax you have to pay by making charitable donations or contributing to a retirement account. Tax laws change and can be very complicated, but not understanding the rules doesn't mean you don't have to follow them. If your business doesn't pay the taxes it owes, the government can shut it down. The IRS may audit (do a

Get It in Writing

While verbal and handshake contracts are legally valid, they are much more difficult to enforce than written ones. When you enter a contract with someone else, you set down the terms of an agreement and are legally bound to complete them. Contracts provide protection for both parties. If one person fails to do what is agreed, then the other can take legal recourse against him. It's important to note, however, that minors (people under age eighteen) cannot legally enter into a contractual agreement. Transactions on the online auction site eBay, for example, involve contracts, and it is illegal for minors to participate in them. Nonetheless, even if a written agreement cannot be enforced in court, it could help clear up points of confusion.

thorough check of) your return several years after you've filed it, so don't throw stuff away as soon as you're done. The rule of thumb is to keep records for seven years.

Making It Work

Once you understand your numbers, you can adjust your budget and your business strategies to increase the bottom line. Pricing is an obvious way to affect your numbers. Compare your prices to what competitors charge. If they're significantly higher, it may drive off potential customers. However, undercharging can also be a mistake. You've got

Tom Siebel, who founded the software company Siebel Systems, is a billionaire today, but it took years of smart spending for him to get there.

to earn enough not only to cover your expenses, but also to make it worth your time.

Some customers will look for the cheapest option, but many believe that "You get what you pay for." If you're providing a quality product or service, price it so that you can make a reasonable profit—after all, that's why you're in business.

The flip side to making money is saving money. "Bootstrapping" is a key strategy for many entrepreneurs. The term comes from the old saying about pulling yourself up by the bootstraps and working with what you have. Smart budgeters look for ways to cut costs without neces- sarily cutting corners. Evaluate where money is being spent. Do you require a data plan on your phone, or do you spend most of your time at home or in the office, where it would be just as easy to check your e-mail without the added cost? Do you require new equipment, or could you purchase it used for the time being? Entrepreneur Tom Siebel, who built the multibillion-dollar company Siebel Systems, reports that when he was starting out, he bought used furniture at auction and rented the cheapest office space he could find.

Look for ways you can piggyback on other people's resources, too. You might be able to open a kiosk in an existing store to sell your scarves for a fraction of the rent that a whole store would cost. Or, you might consider mowing a lawn for free if the owner will allow you to use his mower for other jobs. Also consider trading your ser- vices for ones that you need. Anything that can conserve cash will help your business hold on.

If you have employees, consider the hidden ways they can help. You can pay someone to answer the phone, but what is she doing when it isn't ringing? If she's got Web design skills, then you might put her in charge of keeping up your online presence, saving you the trouble and expense of hiring someone else. If you were paying your phone answerer $8 an hour, you could pay your phone answerer/Web designer $10 an hour—still saving you money, and offering her a better job than she might find elsewhere.

Being frugal is great, but don't fall into the trap of being so cheap that it hampers your ability to do business. If you're always out and about, and your business depends on customers reaching you quickly, then that data plan on your phone might be a legitimate—and smart—expense. Figure out how your customers' money reaches you, and put your money into strategies that will make the flow easier.

Ten Great Questions to Ask a
FINANCIAL ANALYST

1 What are some good strategies to determine whether there's a legitimate market for my business?

2 It's difficult to estimate my start-up costs or project my income. How should I handle the unknowns when I'm presenting to a bank or an investor?

3 Given the nature of my business, what's a reasonable time frame for me to expect to make money?

4 My product or service is unlike anything out there. How can I convince investors it will work?

5 I don't have anything to put up for collateral. Where can I go to get a loan?

6 I don't have my own idea for a business, but I still want to run one. Should I consider a franchise?

7 What legal structure is best for the kind of business I'm starting?

8 What kinds of tax shelters do I qualify for?

9 I can't afford to cut my prices. How can I attract customers and convince them that it's worth the extra money?

10 What are some smart ways to reinvest my profits back into the business? Should I focus on my core business or look for ways to branch out?

Chapter 5

Growing a Business

Markets shift constantly, and most businesses have to adapt to keep up with the times. IBM was known for its typewriters in the 1950s, but eventually the company moved into computers and other technology to stay competitive. As a business's strategies and operations evolve, so will its financial goals.

Revising Goals

The big goal of your company—to make money—isn't one that's likely to change. However, there is more than one way to make money. As you become more familiar with the market, and more comfortable with your own skills, you may adjust the direction you want your company to take. Maybe you've been mowing lawns for families around town. However, an opportunity arises where the local golf course needs a groundskeeper. You could reduce the number of residential jobs in order to free up time and resources to take on the golf course.

In the 1940s, IBM's typewriters were on the cutting edge of technology. But times change, and companies must offer new products to stay competitive.

Perhaps you met your income projections for the first couple of years, but now, having established yourself and your business, you're ready to increase them. That's one approach. On the other hand, you might decide to lower your money-making sights, and instead concentrate on developing another aspect of the business, understanding that it will take time to make this new avenue profitable.

If you've been paying attention to your budget, you've gotten a good sense of what makes money, and what doesn't.

Divide and Conquer

Even though you're running a business to make money for yourself, it's a good idea to keep your business and personal finances separate. For one thing, this makes record keeping easier. You can easily find what you need at tax time, and it makes it clearer to determine how the business is doing. Of course, you can pay yourself a salary if you like—just be sure to record it in the books. Many teen entrepreneurs use the rule of thirds when determining how to use their business earnings: one-third goes back into the business; one-third goes into a savings fund, such as for college; and the final third can be used for fun.

Your original goal might have been to earn most of your money from babysitting. Meanwhile, on the side you offered your pet- and plant-care services for vacationing families. But after a year, it's clear that housesitting pays much better. If you scaled back on the babysitting jobs, you could devote more time to the more profitable aspect of the business.

Your return on investment (ROI) gives you a mathematical calculation of how well you're doing. It shows you what you're getting (return), compared to what you put in (investment). To get the number, first subtract your expenses from your total income (gross profit). The resulting number is your net profit. Now, divide your net profit by what you paid out (your expenses). Multiply that number by 100. Suppose you made $400 in gross profit and spent $200.

Your net profit is $400 minus $200, or $200. Now, divide that number by what you invested, $200, to get 1. Multiply that by 100 and express the result as a percentage. Your return on investment is 100 percent.

Making Changes

Profits are soaring, the phone is ringing off the hook, and customers love you. But where do you go from here? A

Apple Computer has consistently offered new products that appeal to consumers who are willing to pay for creative, convenient entertainment. Some of its products include the wildly popular iPod, iPad, and iPhone.

small business might be able to operate out of the basement, with you as the sole employee. But there may come a time when you've outgrown your original plan. You can't do all the work yourself, but if your idea is unique, and you've established a name for yourself, then you can build on your accomplishments.

Reinvesting in the business is one key strategy for growth. Just as start-up money is needed to get things off the ground, more money is needed to expand your enterprise. You might invest in better equipment, more employees, increasing your marketing and advertising presence, or researching different ways to grow the business. Apple started by making computers, but the company didn't settle for that: instead, it dug deeper and found a new market in iPods.

Some businesses can be franchised. This means that the owner of the business sells the right to someone else to operate the same business type, under the same name, but in a different market (often determined geographically). Chain restaurants are easily recognized franchises, but all kinds of businesses can be franchised. The hair giant Supercuts, for example, and the tax preparation firm H&R Block were both started by entrepreneurs and now have hundreds of franchises across the country.

Remember, however, that trying to grow too quickly has sunk many a business. Reinvesting profits is a tried-and-true approach for building a business's overall worth, but this often means there's no cash available for emergencies or slow periods. There's also the problem of simply taking on too much. Even if you attract new customers, can you do all the work? Hiring employees is one solution, but they may need time to be trained and get up to speed with the way you operate. If you've got too much going on, quality could suffer, which won't please any of your customers—old or new.

Just Say "No"

Or, at least, don't say "yes" immediately. Good business-people understand that making a deal is an art form unto itself, and negotiation is part of the process. If someone offers you a deal that you can't accept, you don't have to shake your head sadly and walk away. Instead, try a counteroffer. Suppliers want your business. If you can't pay their asking price, they might accept a lower one. You can sweeten the deal by offering something in return. Perhaps you'll buy more than you initially had planned. Or, instead of having them deliver the goods, you agree to pick them up. If a customer wants your services but can't afford them, maybe you can accept a lower price on the condition that the job will be a lower priority. You'll fit it in during slow periods. That way, you're still making the most of your available time. Remember not to make your best offer up front. And if you're not willing to accept the terms of the other party, be prepared to walk away.

The truth is, most new businesses fail. It might be a non-marketable idea, or it might come down to poor money management. If, despite your best efforts, your business isn't working, don't make yourself crazy trying to fix it as you go deeper into debt. Cut your losses, learn from your mistakes, and start your next business as a wiser business owner.

If you are successful, remember who helped you get there. Reward good employees with stock options, or a percentage of profits. If they've worked long hours for cut-rate pay, be generous with a bonus when you can afford it.

Exit Strategies

Lots of entrepreneurs think about how they're going to get into business. Very few consider how they're going to get out. At some point, you're probably going to want to do something else, even if it's starting another business.

The New York Stock Exchange is one of several exchanges where stocks are bought and sold. Some businesses raise money by selling shares of the company to the public.

Serious entrepreneurs develop an exit strategy. These plans are important to attract investors, who don't want to invest their money forever. Instead, they want to know when the business will start to reap benefits and when they can harvest the financial rewards.

Although many businesses are run for fun or to provide a living, others are launched specifically with a strategy of growth and an end goal of getting out. At this point, you may not be ready to let your "baby" leave the nest. Nonetheless, it makes sense to think about the end stages of your venture. If the business is well-run and profitable, you might be able to sell it for far more than it cost to start.

Consider, also, that an exit strategy doesn't necessarily mean a complete exit from the business itself. What began as a small, privately owned business could go public by offering shares of stock for sale. The company still exists, but it has changed into another form.

That's the same path that many entrepreneurs follow for themselves. They get a good idea and start a business. Some succeed and others fail. But smart entrepreneurs know how to improve their odds—starting with a solid financial knowledge that will help them take advantage of opportunities, weather the tough times, and build a business that will last.

Glossary

amortize To spread out an expense over a period of time.

audit To thoroughly check and verify financial statements for accuracy.

cash flow statement A record that states actual money that a business has received or spent.

collateral Property promised in return for a loan, which will be surrendered if the loan is not repaid.

debt financing Securing money for a company through borrowing.

depreciate To devalue an asset over time.

equity financing Securing money for a company by offering a stake in the company in return.

fluctuation A variation or change due to outside circumstances.

franchise A business that uses the name and operating procedures of an already existing business.

gross profit The total amount of money that a company brings in.

income statement Also called a profit and loss statement; the revenues and expenses of a company.

invoice A bill; a statement declaring what was purchased and how much money is owed.

liable To be responsible for costs, damages, or wrongdoing.

lucrative Profitable.

net profit The difference between a company's gross profit and its expenses.

niche A specific segment.

overhead General expenses not specifically tied to making a product or service, but necessary to run the business.

profit and loss statement Also called an income statement; the revenues and expenses of a company.

return on investment A figure showing how much was received compared to how much was invested, expressed as a percentage.

tax deductible Describing a cost that can be subtracted from total taxable income.

viability The likelihood that something has to be successful.

For More Information

Canadian Youth Business Foundation (CYBF)
100 Adelaide Street West, Suite 1302
Toronto, ON M5H 1S3
Canada
(866) 646-2922
Web site: http://www.cybf.ca
Programs through the CYBF, as well as personal mentors, help young Canadians start businesses by offering advice and services in planning, financing, and launching a business.

Consortium for Entrepreneurship Education
1601 W. Fifth Avenue, #199
Columbus, OH 43212
(614) 486-6538
Web site: http://www.entre-ed.org
The Consortium encourages education in entrepreneurship in academic and community programs, offering advocacy and leadership support, technical assistance, and other resources.

Internal Revenue Service (IRS)
10th Street and Pennsylvania Avenue NW
Washington, DC 20004
(800) 829-4933
Web site: http://www.irs.gov
This tax-collecting branch of the U.S. government offers assistance to individuals and businesses about tax regulations and filing processes.

Minority Business Development Agency (MBDA)
1401 Constitution Avenue NW
Washington, DC 20230

(202) 482-2332
Web site: http://www.mbda.gov
A branch of the U.S. Department of Commerce, the MBDA
    coordinates public and private resources to encourage
    · the development of businesses owned by minorities.

National Association of Women Business Owners (NAWBO)
601 Pennsylvania Avenue NW
South Building, Suite 900
Washington, DC 20004
(800) 556-2926
Web site: http://nawbo.org
The NAWBO helps promote women business owners by
    promoting economic development among entrepreneurs,
    advocating for policy changes, and building alliances.

National Venture Capital Association (NVCA)
1655 North Fort Myer Drive, Suite 850
Arlington, VA 22209
(703) 524-2549
Web site: http://www.nvca.org
A membership organization for venture capitalists, the NVCA
    advocates for members and entrepreneurs by encouraging
    policies that support innovation and long-term investment.

Network for Teaching Entrepreneurship (NFTE)
120 Wall Street, 18th Floor
New York, NY 10005
Web site: http://www.nfte.com
Founded by an entrepreneur in 1987, the NFTE helps low-
    income youths by teaching entrepreneurship skills they
    can use to help them succeed in business.

Small Business Investor Alliance
1100 H Street NW, Suite 610
Washington, DC 20005
(202) 628-5055
Web site: http://www.nasbic.org
This organization strives to maintain a voice for small business
	investors in government policy, as well as offer network-
	ing and support services.

U.S. Small Business Administration (SBA)
409 3rd Street SW
Washington, DC 20416
(800) 827-5722
Web site: http://www.sba.gov
The SBA advocates for small businesses within the federal
	government. It offers several programs and services,
	including loans, to help small business owners.

Web Sites

Due to the changing nature of Internet links, Rosen Publishing
has developed an online list of Web sites related to the subject
of this book. This site is updated regularly. Please use this link
to access the list:

http://www.rosenlinks.com/GSM/Entre

For Further Reading

Bellenir, Karen, ed. *Cash and Credit Information for Teens: Tips for a Successful Financial Life.* Detroit, MI: Omnigraphics, 2009.

Bellenir, Karen, ed. *Debt Information for Teens: Tips for a Successful Financial Life.* Detroit, MI: Omnigraphics, 2011

Beroff, Art, and T. R. Adams. *How to Be a Teenage Millionaire.* Irvine, CA: Entrepreneur Media, 2000.

Bielagus, Peter. *Quick Cash for Teens: Be Your Own Boss and Make Big Bucks.* New York, NY: Sterling Publishing, 2009.

Bochner, Arthur. *The New Totally Awesome Business Book for Kids.* New York, NY: Newmarket Press, 2007.

Burleson, Kimberly Spinks, and Robyn Collins. *Prepare to Be a Teen Millionaire.* Deerfield Beach, FL: Health Communications, 2008.

Butler, Tamsen. *The Complete Guide to Personal Finance: For Teenagers and College Students.* Ocala, FL: Atlantic Publishing Group, 2010.

Chatzky, Jean. *Not Your Parents' Money Book: Making, Saving, and Spending Your Own Money.* New York, NY: Simon & Schuster Books for Young Readers, 2010.

Ferguson's Careers in Focus: Entrepreneurs. New York, NY: Ferguson, 2009.

Finell, Dorothy. *The Specialty Shop: How to Create Your Own Unique and Profitable Retail Business.* New York, NY: AMACOM, 2007.

Greene, Cynthia. *Entrepreneurship: Ideas in Action.* Mason, OH: South-Western Educational Publishing, 2011.

Karsh, Ellen, and Arlen Sue Fox. *The Only Grant-Writing Book You'll Ever Need: Top Grant Writers and Grant Givers Share Their Secrets.* New York, NY: Basic Books, 2009.

Lesonsky, Rieva. *Start Your Own Business: The Only Start-Up Book You'll Ever Need.* Irvine, CA: Entrepreneur Media, 2007.

Lucas, J. James. *The Teen CEO.* Charleston, SC: CreateSpace, 2011.

Mariotti, Steve. *The Young Entrepreneur's Guide to Starting and Running a Business.* New York, NY: Times Business, 2000.

Rankin, Kenrya, and Eriko Takada. *Start It Up: The Complete Teen Business Guide to Turning Your Passions into Pay.* San Francisco, CA: Zest Books, 2011.

Simons, Rae. *Entrepreneurship.* Broomall, PA: Mason Crest Publishers, 2011.

Solovic, Susan Wilson. *The Girls' Guide to Building a Million-Dollar Business.* New York, NY: AMACOM, 2008.

Stephenson, James. *202 Ways to Make Big Bucks and Stop Mooching Off Your Parents.* Irvine, CA: Entrepreneur Press, 2006.

Swartz, Jon. *Young Wealth: Trade Secrets from Teens Who Are Changing American Business.* San Francisco, CA: Rooftop Publishing, 2006.

Topp, Carol. *Running a Micro Business.* Ambassador Publishing, 2010.

Tracy, John. *Accounting for Dummies.* New York, NY: John Wiley & Sons, 2008.

Vallee, Danielle. *Whiz Teens in Business: Everything You Need to Know to Start Your Business Easily and Successfully.* Charleston, SC: CreateSpace, 2008.

Bibliography

Adams, Bob. *Streetwise Small Business Startup.* Avon, MA: Adams Media, 2002.

Advani, Asheesh. "Can Young Entrepreneurs Get Funding?" Entrepreneur.com, February 13, 2006. Retrieved January 23, 2012 (http://www.entrepreneur.com/article/83690).

Allen, Kathleen. *Entrepreneurship for Dummies.* Foster City, CA: IDG Books Worldwide, 2001.

Berry, Tim. "A Simpler Plan for Startups." Bplans.com. Retrieved January 23, 2012 (http://articles.bplans.com/ writing-a-business-plan/a-simpler-plan-for-start-ups/39).

Caplan, Suzanne. *Streetwise Finance and Accounting: How to Keep Your Books and Manage Your Finances Without an MBA, a CPA, or a Ph.D.* Avon, MA: Adams Media, 2000.

Grunder, Martin. *The Nine Super Simple Steps to Entrepreneurial Success.* Cincinnati, OH: Betterway Books, 2003.

Leach, J. Chris, and Ronald W. Melicher. *Entrepreneurial Finance.* Mason, OH: Thomson South-Western, 2003.

Magos, Alice. "Ask Alice About Budgets." Toolkit.com. Retrieved January 20, 2012 (http://www.toolkit.com/news /newsDetail.aspx?aa=1 &nid=budgets).

Mariotti, Steve, and Caroline Glackin. *Entrepreneurship and Small Business Management.* Boston, MA: Prentice Hall, 2012.

MoreBusiness.com. "How to Track Critical Small Business Financial Numbers." September 9, 2011 (http://www. morebusiness.com/how-to-track-critical-small -business-financial-numbers).

Pakroo, Peri. *The Small Business Start-Up Kit: A Step-by-Step Legal Guide.* Berkeley, CA: NOLO, 2010.

Price, Robert W. *Roadmap to Entrepreneurial Success: Powerful Strategies for Building a High-Profit Business.* New York, NY: AMACOM, 2004.

Ransom, Diana. "Seven Money Mistakes Young Entrepreneurs Make." Entrepreneur.com, August 4, 2011. Retrieved January 24, 2012 (http://www.entrepreneur.com/article /220116).

Rogers, Steven, and Roza Makonnen. *The Entrepreneur's Guide to Finance and Business.* New York, NY: McGraw-Hill, 2003.

Sherman, Andrew J. *Raising Capital.* New York, NY: AMACOM, 2005.

SmallBusinessNotes.com. "Cash Management." Retrieved January 20, 2012 (http://www.smallbusinessnotes.com/ business-finances/cash-management.html).

SmallBusinessNotes.com. "How to Find Financing for Your Business." Retrieved January 20, 2012 (http://www .smallbusinessnotes.com/business-finances/how-to-find -financing-for-your-business.html).

Smith, Richard, and Janet Kiholm Smith. *Entrepreneurial Finance.* New York, NY: John Wiley and Sons, 2000.

Tuchman, Robert. *Young Guns: The Fearless Entrepreneur's Guide to Chasing Your Dreams and Breaking Out on Your Own.* New York, NY: AMACOM, 2009.

Tyson, Eric, and Jim Schell. *Small Business for Dummies.* New York, NY: John Wiley & Sons, 2011.

Urquhart-Brown, Susan. *The Accidental Entrepreneur: 50 Things I Wish Someone Had Told Me About Starting a Business.* New York, NY: AMACOM, 2008.

Index

A

Amazon.com, 23
angel investors, 31

B

"bootstrapping," 42
business, how to choose, 7–9,
    12–13
businesses, types of, 18
business plan, parts of, 16–19

C

cash flow statement, 38, 39
Chappell, Tom and Kate, 9
collateral, 28
contracts, 40
corporations, 18
credit card debt, 28, 33

D

debt financing, 25
Disney, Walt, 4–5
due diligence, 31

E

equity financing, 25, 32–33
exit strategies, 51–52

F

financing, sources of
    banks and lenders, 27–28
    evaluating the choices, 32–33

government loans, 28
investors, 28–31, 33, 52
yourself, friends, and family,
    25–27
Ford, Henry, 5
franchising, 49

G

Gates, Bill, 4
goals
    revising, 45–48
    setting, 13–15, 23–24
government loans, 28
grants, 33
gross profit, 37, 47

I

income statement/projected
    income statement, 21,
    35–37, 38–39
intellectual property, 21

J

Jobs, Steve, 4

M

marketing plan and strategy, 16
market research, 8–9

N

net profit, 37, 47–48
niches, market, 11, 12, 19

About the Author

Diane Bailey has written more than twenty nonfiction books for teens on subjects ranging from sports to states to celebrities. She also writes fiction for both kids and adults, and works as an editor for other children's authors. Bailey has two sons and two dogs, and lives in Kansas.

Photo Credits